Defeated COVID-19 and Healed

TRILOGY

Defeated COVID-19 & Healed

Trilogy Christian Publishers a Wholly Owned Subsidary of Trinity Broadcasting Network

2442 Michelle Drive Tustin, CA 92780

Manufactured in the United States of America

10 9 8 7 6 5 4 3 2 1

Library of Congress Cataloging-in-Publication Data is available.

ISBN: 978-1-63769-912-6
E-ISBN: 978-1-63769-913-3

In Memory of

To those who have been directly affected with the COVID-19 coronavirus disease and have been extremely ill, I, William Vargas, dedicate this book to you. By the grace of God and my faith in Him through Christ, I have totally recovered from it. To those of you still fighting the disease, I encourage you to have faith, think positive, and bring it to God. I know it hasn't been an easy journey, especially after losing loved ones and/or friends, but you must stay strong for yourself and your belief that with God nothing is impossible. He can heal you. Stay strong for your families and friends and reach out to them to let them know how much you really love and appreciate them and what they all mean to you. Don't wait because tomorrow isn't promised to anyone.

I would like you all to know that Jesus wants to make you whole, and He is all we need. Just call upon Him, and He will answer. Before Jesus returned to His heavenly Father, He left us these words of encouragement,

> Come to me, all you who are weary and burdened, and I will give you rest. Take my yoke upon you and learn from me, for I am gentle and humble in heart, and you will find rest for your souls. For my yoke is easy and my burden is light.
>
> —Matthew 11:28-30, NIV

ACKNOWLEDGMENTS

With grateful and humble hearts, Barbara and I take this moment to acknowledge the following:

Thank you to the Church of Christ and family and friends alike for your fasting, prayers, and concerns. You are the real warriors. Your prayers along with ours reached the heavenly throne during this most difficult time. We couldn't have gotten through any of this without your support. Thank you all from the bottom of our hearts to yours.

To those who telephoned, texted, posted on social media, ran errands, and sent gifts and cards, we thank you.

May the God of heaven prosper and multiply your blessings. What an amazing God we serve. All this because of what Jesus did for us two thousand years ago, i.e., "He died on the cross for all humanity" (Matthew 27:1-66).

What a blessing it is to have people like you in our lives. You all rock! You are all exactly what the Scriptures say you are, "In which you shine like stars in the universe" (Philippians 2:15b, NIV).

We love you all very much. May God bless you!

Contents

Foreword

This book is based on my experience during the time I became ill with COVID-19. It was during one of my many stays in the hospital that God prompted me to write this book. Although I was feeling awful, I began to write, holding on to the promise mentioned in the scriptures: "He Himself bore our sins in His body on the tree, so that we might die to sins and live for righteousness; by His wounds you have been healed" (1 Peter 2:24, NIV). I trusted that I would be healed before the publication of this book, and for His glory, I am completely healed.

We all struggle in life; some more than others, but no one is exempt. The good news is that no matter what struggles we must endure when we call on Jesus, He helps us and never looks away. We must call upon Him first and learn to trust Him and lean on Him.

There is power in the name of **JESUS**, and it was with His precious blood that we were redeemed, washed, cleansed, sanctified, forgiven of all sins, and healed (1 John 1:7; Acts 20:28; Romans 3:25-26; Hebrews 12:24; 1 Peter 1:18-19; Isaiah 53:5; and 1 Peter 2:24).

INTRODUCTION

COVID-19 attacked my body and weakened my health. Defeating this virus was the worst disease I have ever had to combat. It has been one of the world's deadliest diseases, but with confidence in the Lord Jesus, I can now say, "I have won this battle against COVID-19 by the precious blood of Jesus Christ."

Before I go any further about my experience with COVID-19, I feel compelled by the Spirit of the Lord to express to you the importance of the death of Jesus Christ, God's Son. It's because of what He did for us (that is, He was put to death by crucifixion for all of us), that I was able to defeat COVID-19. Our salvation depends solely on God's love for us (John 3:16-18). It is not anything we may have done that gets us saved. It's not by our own efforts or works. It's a gift from the Almighty! (Ephesians 2:8-9 and 1 Peter 1:10-12)

If you don't have a personal relationship with Jesus, you are living with no hope and are in danger of losing your soul. Salvation is for everyone that calls upon the name of the Lord. And although God knows that not everyone will seek Him, He still loves them and wants them all saved with eternal life (Romans 10:9-13 and John 3:16-18).

I pray you can all digest the above because it's true; I defeated this disease by believing His Word for me and completely trusting Him and staying positive. How we think is how we speak, and if we're thinking negatively then we're also speaking negatively and vice versa. Our thinking affects everything we do and say, whether positive or negative. It even affects our goals and endeavors. What a hiccup! It's a stumbling block holding us back, not allowing us to move forward. If you find yourselves speaking negative things, then simply rephrase your words by ending them with a positive statement. Stay positive!

We find in Matthew's gospel Jesus' words where He says,

> Each tree is recognized by its own fruit. People do not pick figs from thornbushes, or grapes from briers. The good man brings good things out of the good stored up in his heart, and the evil man brings evil things out of the evil stored up in his heart. For out of the overflow of his heart his mouth speaks.
>
> —Luke 6:44–45, NIV

It is vital that we think and speak positively before engaging in conversations. Positivity allows us to set goals and dream big. It allows us to see a better viewpoint to obstacles and emboldens us to act (James 1:22-26). We should also have faith and believe that God will allow us to reap the fruits of our labors.

Having faith is how we succeed and get ahead in life. James the apostle conveyed a clear message on faith without works being dead. In other words: where there's no deed, there's no fruition. It's simply called "laziness" (James 2:14-26).

It's important we learn to become people of fruition: leaders, role models, and people of faith. You should know that in God's kingdom we are both a chosen people and His royal priesthood (1 Peter 2:9 and Revelation 20:1-6). Understanding what this means gives us a positive outlook. Sometimes, we just need to make a big wide U-turn and bang, we see the light and hit the jackpot. Allow the Holy Spirit's guidance in your lives and begin to prosper according to God's will (Proverbs 1:1-7 and Romans 8:5).

More importantly, secure your names in the book of life. Jesus told His disciples to rejoice that their names were written in the book of life in heaven. May your names be written and found in God's book of life, alongside those of us that already know Him (Exodus 32:32-33, Luke 10:20, and Revelation 20:12-15).

To God be the glory!

Defeated COVID-19 and Healed

As I mentioned in the introduction page, I have won this battle against COVID-19 by the precious blood of Jesus Christ. It was with the Spirit of the Lord that I was victorious, and it was in Jesus' name that I proclaimed my health while I was sick and hospitalized. God's holy Word gave me the strength I needed to hold on to my faith in Christ, knowing that all would be well. His Word gave me courage to live knowing I was in God's hands. I just knew it wasn't my time to depart from this world.

Because God's Word dwelled in me, I defeated the deadliest pandemic disease to ever hit the shores of the United States of America and abroad.

COVID-19 has no power over God's Word, period. I'm so glad I know Jesus.

When I was first rushed to the hospital's emergency room (ER) via the ambulance, they tested me for the coronavirus COVID-19 disease, and I tested positive. I was admitted and spent the next few days hospitalized in Florida.

Two Mini Strokes

COVID-19 first inflicted me with two mini strokes. It attacked two of my tiny vessels (that is, "clogged my vessels") right above the right side of my neck.

After spending three days in the hospital, I was discharged once my vital signs were normal. My cardiologist prescribed blood thinners after my discharge so that I could avoid having anymore strokes. I was able to spend Thanksgiving's Day at home with my wife Barbara and Samson (my Chihuahua). Unfortunately, my breathing did not improve, and I went back to the hospital a few days later. I was admitted once again after being diagnosed with double pneumonia.

- 2 -

Double Pneumonia

Once admitted, doctors were surprised to see me there when, just a few days before, I went home doing well. X-rays taken during the first episode showed no issues with my lungs. The doctors were perplexed at this complication with my lungs. The ER put me on two liters of oxygen because I couldn't breathe on my own. COVID-19 has tested the skills of many in the medical community, and my doctors needed to brainstorm to see what course of action they should take.

I was placed on the third floor which was dedicated to patients strictly with COVID-19. Several doctors with different specialties were assigned to my case, including a neurologist, a cardiologist, a pulmonologist, and several staff physicians whose job it was to make sure proper protocol was followed. After six days of treatment, I was once again stable enough to go home. This time with oxygen, and I was assigned with in-home care where my progress was checked daily.

Third Trip to Emergency Room

A few days later, I had a follow up with my primary doctor. I informed them that the visiting nurse had increased the oxygen level to three liters on the previous visit. The doctor did not feel comfortable with the oxygen level being so high and asked that I return to the hospital. He felt that if I needed such a high amount of oxygen, I needed to be monitored by doctors in the hospital. I complied, and back to the hospital I went. New x-rays were taken, and after spending eight hours in the ER waiting for the results, thank God no new complications showed. I was released at 3 a.m. with the oxygen still at three liters. Once I was home, I dropped the oxygen output to one-and-a-half liters just as the doctor requested.

Fourth Trip to Emergency Room

Days after that third ER visit, things were still not progressing for the better, and I was taken back to the hospital.

I was re-admitted due to difficulty breathing and severe coughing. New CT scans revealed fungus in my lungs. Being on strong doses of steroids for over two months had left my immune system vulnerable to bacteria. Along with the fungus in my lungs, I also developed oral thrush, frequent nose bleeds, and sensitive gums. This trip to the hospital had me feeling weak, exhausted, and winded all the time.

This last episode in the hospital was for another nine days. A New Year had begun, and I felt hopeful and relieved that I was finally going home for good.

Recovery

A few days later after being discharged, I started feeling a little relief from the tightness in my chess and my breathing slowly started to improve. Having double pneumonia is debilitating and is a scary thing not to be able to breath. Lucky for me, during this last episode, I no longer required the need for oxygen. My oxygen levels had improved significantly, and slowly I regained my weight and strength. The coughing took the longest to go away—about six to seven months. I was well on my way to recovery and things were looking hopeful and promising. For some it takes longer to heal than for others.

- 3 -

ALL THINGS ARE POSSIBLE WITH GOD

Along the way, I continued to believe God's Word for healing and, with Jesus at the front wheel, I knew for sure I would recover. Prayers were constantly being presented to the Lord on my behalf by Barbara, the Church of Christ, relatives, and friends.

As a Christian man, I have always been a fighter, and I wasn't about to let Satan have his way with me. God had me in His hands, and I had the complete confidence in Him that I would indeed walk away from this alive and well. There was just no room for doubt.

It is true that at times things may seem hard or impossible for us, but not for God (Jeremiah 32:17, Jeremiah 32:26-27, and Matthew 19:16-26).

- 4 -

NIGHTMARES AND INSOMNIA

One of the things I struggled with throughout the duration of the disease was the fact that Satan attacked my sleep with nightmares. These nightmares would occur within the first minute or so after falling asleep, and although I've had nightmares in the past, never with the frequency that I had during the time I was sick with COVID-19.

All these nightmares came from a spirit of persecution. In each dream I found myself either running and/or trying to push my way through a crowd of people. There was one dream that stood out:

A young girl was speaking while I followed the sound of her voice. I didn't know who she was, nor did I see her, I could only hear her voice. Her voice led me out of an apartment building, so I walked across the street to where Barbara was waiting in line to enter a store. Suddenly, a demon appeared in the shape of a woman and stood in front of Barbara, making her disappear, as well as the young girl's voice. This demon then grabbed me, and we began to have a spiritual battle. I fought back by quoting Scriptures and stating the name of Jesus before finally waking up.

Along with the nightmares, I was having bouts of insomnia. The doctors had me on a very high dosage of steroids for more than three months and that contributed to not being able to sleep. Proper sleep helps with a quick recovery not only of the body but also the mind; and Satan tried to prolong my weak state. Satan knows exactly where, when, and how to attack a person's health, especially when he knows we are feeling sick, weak, and most vulnerable. However, God gave me the strength to fight off these obstacles, and slowly my sleep improved.

Nightmares are demonic attacks, and they come directly from Satan and his minions (that is, falling angels or evil spirits). If you struggle with these kinds of nightmares, try applying biblical verses in your prayers before going to bed to help you win these spiritual battles against the devil (James 4:7 and Psalms 4:8).

Significant Weight Loss

COVID-19 caused me to lose a significant amount of weight. I started out at 186 pounds and ended weighing 167 pounds in a matter of three months. I felt tired and weak but grateful that God wasn't finished with me yet.

- 5 -

GOD'S TIMING IS ALWAYS PERFECT

While I was hospitalized, a relative in another state fell ill due to COVID-19 and was hospitalized around Thanksgiving also fighting for his life. We informed our church family of his situation and lifted him up in prayer. Although I wasn't feeling well, I kept in contact with him via texts, social media, and calls. I encouraged him to seek Jesus. Having each other during this time drew us closer. Finally, my relative walked through the door of salvation and accepted Jesus as his Lord and Savior. For years, my relative had heard about Jesus but hadn't taken the step toward salvation.

It humbles me to know that God used me and this sickness to bring him to Jesus. God's timing is never too late.

- 6 -

EXAMINING OURSELVES SPIRITUALLY

While lying in the hospital bed, I thought about my life and my shortcomings. I asked the Lord to cleanse me of any sins that I might not have been aware of.

There may be sins that are not obvious to you and asking God to clean you allows the Holy Spirit to work in your life. Trusting that the Lord knows all things and believing in redemption allows the cleansing of the heart:

> I will be careful to lead a blameless life —
> when will you come to me?
> I will walk in my house
> with blameless heart.
> I will set before my eyes
> no vile thing.
>
> —Psalms 101:2-3, NIV

Search me, God, and know my heart; test me and know my anxious thoughts. See if there is any offensive way in me and lead me in the way everlasting.

—Psalms 139:23–24, TLB

- 7 -

HELL AND THE LAKE OF FIRE

While reading the Book of Acts, I felt the Holy Spirit guiding me to revisit Luke 16:19-31, the Parable of the Rich Man and Lazarus. In this parable, the rich man begs Abraham to send Lazarus to his brothers and warn them about hell. Abraham replies that the living had the writings of Moses and the prophets. The rich man states that presenting someone who has risen from the dead would be more convincing to his family because seeing is better than believing. The rich man's answer reveals a problem that has plagued humans for a long time—that it's too hard to believe in what is not seen.

The parable inferred a couple of things that may not be obvious. One, Abraham was the one who spoke to the rich man and spoke of the scriptures that were given to Moses, a man who did not appear until a few hundred years after Abraham's death. The other was the mention of Abraham's bosom. The bosom was a place that the Jews in Jesus' time understood to mean as a place where the righteous dead went. Abraham, Moses, and the prophets would be among those that were there. When Abraham was alive, the law of Moses was not penned yet and Israel did not exist at the time. Abraham was here first, and he was the grandfather of the Jewish nation, aligning him as Moses' ancestor.

I believe it means when Moses died, he went to Abraham's bosom. There he explained to Abraham and to all those waiting there with him everything the Lord God had done and accomplished for Israel through him. Otherwise, this parable just wouldn't make any kind of sense. And if you will, for no other reason at all, Luke was compelled to write it down as told to him by eyewitness accounts of Jesus' deeds and sayings. This was what I believe the Spirit of the Lord showed me as He redirected me to revisit these scriptural passages.

I believe there is an afterlife and that paradise and hell do exist. There are things written in the scriptures that are impossible to ignore, and this is just one of them. Jesus never gave parables just to give them. There was always a teaching to each of His parables, and there's no doubt in my mind that He wanted His disciples to grasp the meaning.

If you don't believe in the afterlife, then I recommend you read about the transfiguration where it clearly demonstrates Elijah and Moses on the mount with Jesus while three of His disciples saw the vision. Keep in mind that Elijah had been carried by a whirlwind into heaven after a chariot of fire appeared while he was walking with Elisha, and Moses died, and God buried him. This was something that happened way before Jesus' time (Deuteronomy 34:1-8, 2 Kings 2:1-11, and Matthew 17:1-9).

More Scriptures on Hell

Hell does exist for all the ungodly (Jude 1-14)
Lake of Fire (Revelation 19:20)
Judgment Day and the Lake of Fire (Revelation 20:11-15)

- 8 -

MARRIAGE

I reflected a lot on my marriage during the time I had COVID-19.

It's important to respect our marriage vows and the covenant we made before God. Just like Christ loves His church, we men are to love our wives (Ephesians 5:22-33).

My Wife Barbara, A Woman of Valor

The night I fell ill, Barbara woke up to me falling to the floor and nonresponsive. She immediately called for an ambulance. She later told me that she knew that she had to stay calm in order to take charge since I was not in any shape to talk to the EMT and the hospital staff. Once she was alone, she broke down. God knew all the tears and heartache she felt throughout my hospital stay and throughout my recovery.

Barbara is unique like no other. She's an amazing woman and wife to me and a blessing from the Lord God (Proverbs 18:22).

She is a lady of valor and integrity, and I'm blessed and honored to be married to her. I am reminded of a wonderful verse that sums up Barbara's attributes. And the verse says,

"Many women do noble things, but you surpass them all." Charm is deceptive, and beauty is fleeting; but a woman who fears the Lord is to be praised. Give her the reward she has earned, and let her works bring her praise at the city gate.

—Proverbs 31:29-31, NIV

- 9 -

Worshiping and Praising the King—JESUS

Staying in constant praise and worship was key for my healing! Death never entered my thoughts while I was hospitalized, not even once. As I lay sick in the hospital, every single day I raised my hands up toward heaven and sang praises to God and thanked Him for everything. The importance of praising God with song is something I learned while playing guitar with a worship team in New Jersey.

Praising God gives us peace of mind and comfort. Even when the weakest of Christians lift their voices in praise, Satan must flee.

It was this weapon that kept me believing even when I saw the circumstances surrounding me were bleak. As my praise strengthened, so did my faith and confidence. Once I was discharged, I continued the same routine of praise and worship (1 Samuel 16:14-23, James 4:7-10, and 2 Samuel 22:1-7).

While in the hospital the Holy Spirit ministered to my heart about writing my story. I had no intentions of writing another book; however, God had other plans.

God's healing power is real, and it works. Commence by singing to Him hymns and songs of praise. I pray this edifies believers everywhere. This truth is for everyone seeking His healing power and is something I'm still seeking for other parts of my body that have nothing to do with COVID-19. I will continue confessing and believing and declaring healing with praises to the Lord God.

The Armor of God

Take time out to study God's Word. It's mostly how God will be talking to your heart and the Holy Spirit will direct your paths. Think of God's Word as if showering with soap and water. We are refreshed because it cleanses us and makes us smell and feel good. It's like a fragrance—you must apply it to smell good. That's how God's Word together with the Holy Spirit works in our lives. And it's how one becomes born again after first giving your heart to Christ (John 3:3-8, 1 Peter 1:23, and 1 Peter 2:1-3).

Humbled

Dealing with COVID-19 has been a humbling experience. No matter how much I prayed against contamination, it happened without my consent and with such a fury. It had me thinking about a verse that says, "My days are like the evening shadow; I wither away like grass" (Psalms 102:11, NIV).

Praying in the Holy Spirit

As a Christian, it's important that you have a prayer life. Praying in the Spirit is one of the most powerful ways a believer can pray. It was what helped me fight off the demons of nightmares, and God's mercy was upon me. Speaking in tongues is a believer's tool against all demonic forces. And as believers, we don't need to wait for God to turn on a switch. It is a gift given freely to those who want it. It is through prayer and asking that the gift will come. That's how I received it many years ago. (Ephesians 6:10-18—focus on verse eighteen for praying.)

Learn to become praying warriors of God's Word by quoting biblical verses when praying. Praying with His Word is praying according to His will (1 Corinthians 12:1-31 for the gifts of the Spirit).

- 10 -

NUTRITION

One of the side-effects of having COVID-19 was the loss of taste. No matter what I ate, everything tasted horrible. Fortunately, I didn't lose my appetite and was able to have snacks between meals.

Satan's Attack Against My Body and Mind

Satan knows the time he has on earth is short, and he does everything he can to destroy our lives. I believe his hand is on COVID-19, which has tested the faith of many believers who don't see the spiritual battle behind this sickness.

Lying in bed can make you feel worse mentally, and I knew that if I sat in a chair or walked a few steps that I would feel better and push back the negative thoughts and depression that tried to plague me. And because of COVID-19, hospital visits were not allowed, making things more depressing. So, I would speak the Word out loud and visualize the healing come over me. I would tell myself that God had intervened by telling Satan that I was purchased with the precious blood of Jesus, and he couldn't take my life. (1 Peter 1:18-21, John 10:10, and 1 Thessalonians 5:16-18)

Learn to Be Your Own Advocate

Learn to be your own advocate and be aware of your medications and your health conditions. Whether you're at home or in the hospital, always pay close attention and know what the doctors, nurses, and staff are always administering to you. Don't be afraid to ask questions, remembering that doctors are only human. Keep your family informed of any changes with your health and medications. Know what you need, when you need it, and why you need it.

God's Holy Word

For the word of God is living and active. Sharper than any double-edged sword, it penetrates even to dividing soul and spirit, joints and marrow; it judges the thoughts and attitudes of the heart. Nothing in all creation is hidden from God's sight. Everything is uncovered and laid bare before the eyes of him to whom we must give account.

—Hebrews 4:12–13,

Thank You Father God, thank You Jesus, and thank You Holy Spirit. I have praised You and given You all the glory!

Shalom

Pray for the peace of Jerusalem:
"May those who love you be secure.
May there be peace within your walls
and security within your citadels."
For the sake of my brothers and friends,
I will say, "Peace be within you."
For the sake of the house of the Lord our God,
I will seek your prosperity.

—Psalms 122:6-9, NIV

"Jesus is Messiah"